$\mathcal{A}$ gift for:

$\mathcal{F}$rom:

$\mathcal{D}$ate:

God's
LITTLE
PROMISE
BOOK
FOR
Graduates

J. COUNTRYMAN®

All Scripture quotations in this book are from the
New King James Version (nkjv) ©1979, 1980, 1982, 1992,
Thomas Nelson, Inc., Publisher and are used by permission.

Compiled by Luke V. Gibbs and Terri Gibbs

Designed by Starletta Polster Design, Murfreesboro, Tennessee

ISBN: 0-8499-9565-5

www.jcountryman.com

Printed and bound in Mexico

Congratualations

$\mathcal{A}$t every choice, every crossroads, every doubt—let God be your guide.

---

*My God shall supply all your need
according to His riches in glory by Christ Jesus.*
PHILIPPIANS 4:19

*N*o pleasure is without its cost.
Be sure you check the price tag.

If you keep My commandments, you will abide
in My love, just as I have kept
My Father's commandments and abide in His love.
JOHN 15:9

In a world of bravado and compromise, the Word of God is an oasis of sanity and joy.

Every word of God is pure;
He is a shield to those who put their trust in Him.
PROVERBS 30:5

*P*erseverance, like a pearl,
is priceless.

———

Be patient, brethren,
until the coming of the Lord. . . .
Indeed we count them blessed
who endure.
JAMES 5:7, 11

*G*od's love, like a lamp,
is most visible
in the darkest hours.

Behold, the LORD's *hand is not shortened,*
that it cannot save; nor His ear heavy,
that it cannot hear.
ISAIAH 59:1

*S*uccess in any relationship
calls for each to give 100 percent
to the other.

———

Be of good comfort, be of one mind, live in peace;
and the God of love and peace will be with you.
2 CORINTHIANS 13:11

Be careful what you bring
into your mind.
It just might grow there.

Commit your works to the LORD,
and your thoughts will be established.
PROVERBS 16:3

13

*H*ow to confront problems?
Perseve and pray.

—

Then you will call upon Me and go and pray to Me,
and I will listen to you.
JEREMIAH 29:12

*S*uccess is more about what
you become on the inside than what
you accomplish on the outside.

The counsel of the LORD stands forever,
the plans of His heart to all generations.
PSALM 33:11

*T*he greatest failure is
the failure to try.

———

The LORD will guide you continually,
and satisfy your soul in drought . . . ;
you shall be like a watered garden,
and like a spring of water,
whose waters do not fail.
ISAIAH 58:11

One of the keys to financial
success is to learn
quickly that enough is enough.

—

I have learned in whatever state I am, to be content.
PHILIPPIANS 4:11

$\mathcal{B}$e the person who dreams
of lifetime achievements and works
hard to make them come true.

Ask, and it will be given to you;
seek, and you will find;
knock, and it will be opened to you.
MATTHEW 7:7

$\mathcal{P}$eople will enjoy being around
you if you make them feel significant.

———

Be kind to one another, tenderhearted,
forgiving one another,
even as God in Christ forgave you.
EPHESIANS 4:32

*S*ervant leaders (successful leaders)
want to make others feel important.

———

God resists the proud,
but gives grace to the humble.
1 PETER 5:5

$\mathcal{P}$erseverance is one of the
most important traits to develop
for success in every area of life.

I love those who love me,
and those who seek me diligently will find me.
PROVERBS 8:17

*L*earn to look at obstacles
as opportunities.

---

*Delight yourself also in the LORD;
and He shall give you the desires of your heart.*
PSALM 37:4

$\mathcal{W}$hen you feel overwhelmed
by work, step back.
Then relax, reflect, and focus
on positive steps toward progress.

Cast your burden on the LORD,
and he shall sustain you;
He shall never permit the righteous to be moved.
PSALM 55:22

*H*old onto the dream
in your heart.
It is God's gift to you.

———

Jesus said to him, "If you can believe,
all things are possible to him who believes."
MARK 9:23

*P*eople of integrity set a
high standard for themselves . . .
and follow it.

———

*Let your light so shine before men,
that they may see your good works and
glorify your Father in heaven.*
MATTHEW 5:16

$\mathcal{D}$on't let your happiness
depend on the perfection of others.

But now God has set the members,
each one of them,
in the body just as He pleased.
1 CORINTHIANS 12:18

$\mathcal{B}$e yourself. Be authentic.

But you are a chosen generation,
a royal priesthood, a holy nation,
His own special people.
1 PETER 2:9

*W*hen life gets complicated,
take time to be silly.

He who heeds the word wisely
will find good,
and whoever trusts in the LORD,
happy is he.
PROVERBS 16:20

*W*hen temptation comes,
ask God to show you the exit.
Then walk through it!

—

But the Lord is faithful,
who will establish you
and guard you from the evil one.
2 THESSALONIANS 3:3

*A*void the trap of having plenty
and wanting plenty more.

Better is a little with the fear of the LORD,
than great treasure with trouble.
PROVERBS 15:16

*A*lways be eager to applaud others,
to pat them on the back.
You'll never lack for friends.

Behold how good and
how pleasant it is for brethren
to dwell together in unity!

$\mathcal{Y}$ou will always find yourself
when you lose yourself
for the sake of others.

———

*God is able to make all grace abound
toward you, that you . . .
may have an abundance for every good work.*
2 CORINTHIANS 9:8

*A*t the core of all sin is pride.

He who is proud of heart
stirs up strife,
but he who trusts in the LORD
will be prospered.
PROVERBS 28:25

*W*hen we feel we need God least,
we need Him most.

—

Jesus said to them, "I am the bread of life.
He who comes to Me shall never hunger,
and he who believes in Me shall never thirst."
JOHN 6:35

*K*eep your confidence in God.
He will never let you down.

——

The LORD is my light and my salvation;
whom shall I fear?
PSALM 27:1

A life outside of God
is no life at all.

*For the Son of Man has come to seek
and to save that which was lost.*
LUKE 19:10

*W*here we can't walk,
God can teach us to fly.

Those who wait on the LORD
shall renew their strength;
they shall mount up
with wings like eagles. . . .
ISAIAH 40:31

*R*egardless how fierce
the storm, you can always find
shelter in God's love.

Peace I leave with you, My peace I give to you;
not as the world gives do I give to you.
Let not your heart be troubled, neither let it be afraid.
JOHN 14:27

*G*od gathers the remnants
of your life and weaves them into
a work of dignity and purpose.

———

He who has begun a good work in you
will complete it until the day of Jesus Christ.
PHILIPPIANS 1:6

*W*e fear what we don't know,
don't understand, or can't control.
Leave your fear with the
One who knows, understands,
and controls all things.

———

The LORD shall preserve your going out
and your coming in . . . even forevermore.
PSALM 121:8

*N*o insult ever achieved peace.

There is one who speaks like the
piercings of a sword, but the tongue of
the wise promotes health.
PROVERBS 12:18

Work, like everything else
in this world, is temporary.
Don't determine your self worth by
what you do but by who you are.

*Therefore be imitators of God as dear children.
And walk in love. . . .*
EPHESIANS 5:1–2

*S*omehow, those who give away
the most are never in need.

———

Give, and it will be given to you:
good measure, pressed down, shaken together,
and running over, will be put into your bosom.
For with the same measure that you use,
it will be measured back to you.
LUKE 6:38

*W*hen one door is closed,
another opens.
God always directs us,
even when we can't
see the final destination.

———

To everything there is a season,
a time for every purpose under heaven.
ECCLESIASTES 3:1

$\mathcal{B}$efore you face the challenges
of your day, face the day with God.

He who dwells in the secret place
of the Most High shall abide under
the shadow of the Almighty.
PSALM 91:1

*Y*ou can learn from success,
but you'll probably learn
more from failure and disappointment.

———

Fear not, for I am with you;
be not dismayed, for I am your God.
I will strengthen you, yes, I will help you,
I will uphold you with My righteous right hand.
ISAIAH 41:10

*N*ever let the clatter and chatter
of the day-to-day
drown out God's words.

———

Heaven and earth shall pass away,
but My words will by no means pass away.
MARK 13:31

A gentle word can
defuse a situation;
a sharp word will ignite it.

—

Pleasant words are like a honeycomb,
sweetness to the soul and health to the bones.
PROVERBS 16:24

*W*isdom is being aware of your limitations, yet confident of God's unlimited love and power.

—

The steps of a good man are ordered by the LORD and He delights in his way.
PSALM 37:23

49

*I*n a world where blind guides
lead the unsuspecting to oblivion,
God promises to give both
sight and insight.

I will instruct you and teach you
in the way you should go;
I will guide you with My eye.
PSALM 32:8

*W*hen you give,
you please two people.

*A generous man devises generous things,
and by generosity he shall stand.*
Isaiah 32:8

*N*ever settle for rags when God
has promised you riches.

Therefore, if anyone is in Christ,
he is a new creation; old things have passed away;
behold all things have become new.
2 CORINTHIANS 5:17

*I*n Jesus, we give up the worthless
for the priceless.

I, even I, am He who
blots out your transgressions for My own sake;
and I will not remember your sins.
ISAIAH 43:25

*A*n education is never finished, whether it is in books or in the Book.

How can a young man cleanse his way?
By taking heed according to Your word.
PSALM 119:9

$\mathcal{T}$he end of your power is
just the beginning of God's power.

God has not given us a spirit of fear,
but of power and of love and of a sound mind.
2 TIMOTHY 1:7

$\mathcal{A}$ll work—any work—
can be done to glorify God.

Whatever your hand finds to do,
do it with your might.
ECCLESIASTES 9:10

*Y*ou only value God
at all when you
value Him above all.

Now to the King eternal, immortal, invisible,
to God who alone is wise,
be honor and glory forever and ever.
1 TIMOTHY 1:17

$\mathcal{T}$rust the all-seeing eyes
of your gracious God to help you
in every area of your life.

———

For the eyes of the LORD run to and fro
throughout the whole earth,
to show Himself strong on behalf of those
whose heart is loyal to Him.
2 CHRONICLES 16:9

$\mathcal{Y}$ou don't have to take a
number with God. You
are always at the head of the line.

━━━

Then the King will say to those on His right hand,
"Come, you blessed of My Father,
inherit the kingdom prepared for you from the
foundation of the world."
MATTHEW 25:34

*G*od wants to be your
first choice—
not your last resort.

May our God and Father Himself . . .
establish your hearts
blameless in holiness before [Him].
1 THESSALONIANS 3:11–13

*G*od forgets the past,
clears the present,
and opens tomorrow.

———

Let the peace of God rule in your hearts,
to which also you were
called in one body; and be thankful.
COLOSSIAN 3:15

*A*lways let humility and
kindness feel welcome in your heart.

*The fruit of the Spirit is love, joy, peace,
longsuffering, kindness, goodness, faithfulness,
gentleness, self-control.*
GALATIANS 5:22–23

*T*he tree with deep roots
weathers the hurricane. With roots
deep in God's Word you
can weather the storms of life.

All scripture is given by inspiration of God,
and is profitable for doctrine, for reproof,
for correction, for instruction in righteousness.
2 TIMOTHY 3:16

*I*n the end, what will matter
is not only what God did in us,
but what He did through us.

Let us not grow weary
while doing good,
for in due season we shall reap
if we do not lose heart.
GALATIANS 6:9

$\mathcal{T}$he life of faith is a laboratory course, not a lecture. Put the Bible to the test and watch it work.

———

For the word of God is living and powerful,
and sharper than any two-edged sword,
piercing even to the division of soul and spirit,
and of joints and marrow, and is a
discerner of the thoughts and intents of the heart.
HEBREWS 4:12

$\mathcal{G}$od believes in you more than
you believe in yourself.

How precious also are
Your thoughts to me, O God!
How great is the sum of them!
PSALM 139:17

*E*ntrust your troubles to God.
He'd be disappointed if you didn't.

Trust in the LORD with all your heart,
and lean not on your own understanding;
in all your ways acknowledge Him,
and He shall direct your paths.
PROVERBS 3:5–6

*R*eligion is easy;
a godly life isn't.

---

*I will instruct you and teach you
in the way you should go;
I will guide you with My eye.*
PSALM 32:8

*P*eer pressure can run you
off the path or keep you on it.
Choose your friends wisely.

———

He who walks with wise men will be wise,
but the companion of fools will be destroyed.
PROVERBS 13:20

$\mathcal{T}$he only time God doesn't
answer is when He isn't called.

———

He shall call upon Me,
and I will answer him;
I will be with him in trouble;
I will deliver him and honor him.
PSALM 91:15

$\mathcal{W}$e think most about what is
closest to our hearts.

—

Whatever things are true,
whatever things are noble,
whatever things are just,
whatever things are pure,
whatever things are lovely,
whatever things are of good report,
if there is any virtue and if anything
praiseworthy—meditate on these things.
PHILLIPIANS 4:8

*G*od is the author of every day—
every minute, every hour.

And we know that all things work
together for good to those who love God,
to those who are the
called according to His purpose.
ROMANS 8:28

Be firm in what you stand for
and leery of what you fall for.

*There is a way that seems right to a man,
but its end is the way of death.*
PROVERBS 14:12

*N*othing is as hollow as a
life empty of God.

—

Abide in Me, and I in you.
As the branch cannot bear fruit of itself,
unless it abides in the vine,
neither can you, unless you abide in Me.
JOHN 15:4

A true friend will tell
you what's right and what's wrong.

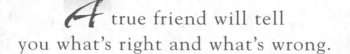

By this all will know that you are My disciples,
if you have love for one another.
JOHN 13:35

*G*od wants to have a
permanent place in your heart.

—

Behold, I stand at the door and knock.
If anyone hears My voice and opens the door,
I will come in to him and dine with him,
and he with Me.
REVELATION 3:20

*F*rom discipline come
strength and courage.

The LORD will give grace and glory;
no good thing will He withhold from those
who walk uprightly.
PSALM 84:11

*G*od gave you His only Son.
What wouldn't He give you?

For by grace you have been
saved through faith,
and that not of yourselves;
it is the gift of God, not of works,
lest anyone should boast.
EPHESIANS 2:8–9

$\mathcal{T}$here's much more power
in an open hand
than a clenched fist.

The merciful man does good for his own soul.
PROVERBS 11:17

The largest room in the world
is the room for improvement.

That you, always having all
sufficiency in all things,
may have an abundance for
every good work.
2 CORINTHIANS 9:8

A life of virtue is a
life worth living.
A life of pleasure is wearisome
and tedious.

He who keeps instruction is in the way of life,
but he who refuses correction goes astray.
PROVERBS 10:17

*G*uilt is God's burglar alarm. Don't let Satan steal your peace of mind.

———

For the wages of sin is death, but the gift of God is eternal life in Christ Jesus our Lord.
Romans 6:23

*K*indness and goodness
speak your faith more loudly
than a thousand platitudes.

A man has joy
by the answer of his mouth,
and a word spoken in due season,
how good it is!
PROVERBS 15:23

*G*od created all of the
earth for you.
Praise Him for His gifts!

———

You are worthy, O Lord,
to receive glory and honor and power;
for You created all things,
and by Your will they exist and were created.
REVELATION 4:11

84

*T*he Lord of lords,
and King of kings,
wants to hear from you!

---

*Let us therefore come boldly
to the throne of grace,
that we may obtain mercy and
find grace to help in time of need.*
HEBREWS 4:16

A word misspoken is
nonrefundable.

No man can tame the tongue.
It is an unruly evil, full of deadly poison.
JAMES 3:8

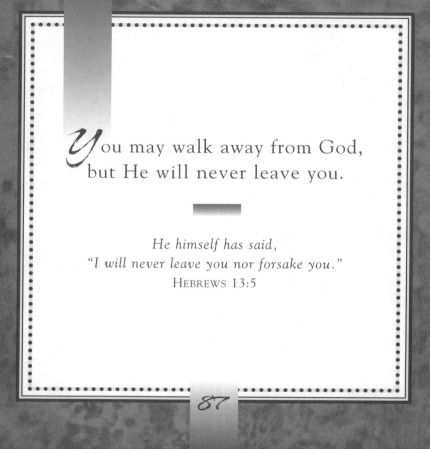

*Y*ou may walk away from God,
but He will never leave you.

—

He himself has said,
"I will never leave you nor forsake you."
HEBREWS 13:5

*N*othing costs as little or
is worth as much as compassion.

———

Beloved, if God so loved us,
we also ought to love one another.
1 JOHN 4:11

*T*he baubles of this world mean
nothing in the next.

—

Let your conduct be without covetousness;
be content with such things as you have.
HEBREWS 13:5

*I*f a godly life is your goal,
the Bible must be your roadmap.

*Your word I have hidden in my heart,
that I might not sin against You.*
PSALM 119:11

*Y*our life isn't an accident.
You are God's gift to the world!

I will praise You,
for I am fearfully and wonderfully made;
marvelous are Your works,
and that my soul knows very well.
PSALM 139:14

$\mathcal{T}$he Word of God has outlived
centuries of critics and
scoffers. It will outlive them
for centuries to come.

———

Heaven and earth will pass away,
but My words will by no means pass away.
MATTHEW 24:35

*W*hile it's important to make
a living, with God you
can know how to make a life.

If you love Me, keep my commandments.
He who has My commandments
and keeps them, it is he who loves Me.
JOHN 14:15, 21

*S*ometimes God's answer
to prayer isn't "yes" or "no,"
but "wait."

Whatever we ask we receive from Him,
because we keep His commandments
and do those things that are pleasing in His sight.
1 JOHN 3:22

The one screaming for
God's justice drowns out His words.
Be still and listen.

It is good that one should hope and
wait quietly for the salvation of the LORD.
LAMENTATIONS 3:26

95

$\mathcal{W}$hen you absolutely have to,
you will find that you can.

I will lift up my eyes to the hills—
from whence comes my help?
PSALM 121:1

*O*nce you endure
the hard times,
you have more joy
in the good times.

Weeping may endure for a night,
but joy comes in the morning.
PSALM 30:5

$\mathcal{Y}$our words are the pen
of your heart.

---

*The mouth of the righteous
is a well of life. . . .
Wisdom is found on the lips of him
who has understanding.*
PROVERBS 10:11, 13

A good time to learn
from your mistakes
is before they happen.

He who is slow to anger is better
than the mighty,
and he who rules his spirit than
he who takes a city.
PROVERBS 16:32

*P*rayer is offering to God
all that your heart holds.

We love him because He first loved us.
1 JOHN 4:19

*T*he formula is simple:
You cannot do God's work,
and He will not do yours.

As for God, his way is perfect;
the word of the LORD is proven;
He is a shield to all who trust in Him.
PSALM 18:30

101

$\mathcal{T}$here are two keys to
getting along with everyone:
be kind, be considerate.

Let your gentleness be known to all men.
PHILIPPIANS 4:5

*M*ake it your goal to
get to know God
a little better every day.

Whoever desires to come after me,
let him deny himself,
and take up his cross, and follow Me.
MARK 8:34

*G*od's will for your life
will bring joy and fulfillment.

The LORD your God in your midst,
the Mighty One, will save;
He will rejoice over you with gladness.
ZEPHANIAH 3:17

*G*od has promised to guide
you if you'll let Him.

Who walks in darkness and has no light?
Let him trust in the name of
the LORD and rely upon his God.
ISAIAH 50:10

$\mathcal{E}$ven the smoothest path in life
has some stones on it.

---

*Behold, I am with you
and will keep you wherever you go.*
GENESIS 28:15

$\mathcal{L}$ive today well and you'll have hope for tomorrow.

——

We know that when He is revealed,
we shall be like Him,
for we shall see Him as He is.
1 JOHN 3:2

*T*he love you give to others
is the love that
will come back to you.

Love one another fervently
with a pure heart.
1 PETER 1:22

*T*he little things in life
are often the best.

The LORD takes pleasure in
those who fear Him,
in those who hope in His mercy.
PSALM 147:11

*I*f you think you can,
with God's help you will.

—

I can do all things through Christ
who strengthens me.
PHILIPPIANS 4:13

$\mathcal{T}$oday's troubles are
tomorrow's anecdotes.
Today's worries are
tomorrow's strengths.

Knowing that the testing of your
faith produces patience.
But let patience have its perfect work,
that you may be perfect and complete,
lacking nothing.
JAMES 1:3–4

*G*od extends mercy
to the miserable,
deliverance to the downtrodden.

A merry heart makes a cheerful countenance,
but by sorrow of the heart the spirit is broken.
PROVERBS 15:13

A lifetime of worry isn't worth
a moment of contentment.

—

Do not worry about tomorrow,
for tomorrow will worry about its own things.
Sufficient for the day is its own trouble.
MATTHEW 6:34

A compliment is heard louder
than a complaint.

The lips of the righteous know
what is acceptable,
but the mouth of the wicked
what is perverse.
PROVERBS 10:32

*T*o resist evil you must turn
away from it!
Say no. Run away!

Therefore submit to God.
Resist the devil and he will flee from you.
JAMES 4:7

*Y*ou can live and learn;
you can also listen and learn.

Give instruction to a wise man,
and he will be still wiser; teach a just man,
and he will increase in learning.

PROVERBS 9:9

Commitment to God
means believing
He is who He says He is,
and acting on it.

■

Whoever confesses that Jesus is the Son of God,
God abides in him, and he in God.
1 JOHN 4:15

*G*od sees the transgressions
in the shadows as easily as
those in the sunshine.
The good news is—He forgives both.

If we confess our sins,
He is faithful an just to forgive us our sins. . . .
1 JOHN 1:9

*P*leasure is temporary.
Satisfaction is fleeting.
The joy of the Lord is eternal.

___

*Let all those rejoice who
put their trust in You;
let them ever shout for joy.*
PSALM 5:11

*M*ake new friends, but
keep the old.

———

Beloved, let us love one another,
for love is of God.
1 John 4:7

$\mathcal{L}$ife is made entirely
of moments multiplied,
as little streamlets, joining,
form the ocean's tide.

—Anonymous

*I must work the works of Him who
sent Me while it is day;
the night is coming when no one can work.*
JOHN 9:4

*W*orry makes mountains
out of molehills.
God makes molehills
out of mountains.

Great is the LORD,
and greatly to be praised in
the city of our God,
in His holy mountain.
PSALM 48:1

*W*e cannot follow the Shepherd
if we insist on leading the way.

—

*Walk in all the ways
that I have commanded you,
that it may be well with you.*
JEREMIAH 7:23

*G*od does not promise us
a life of joyous circumstances.
He promises joy
in the circumstances.

That you may walk worthy of the Lord . . .
strengthened with all might,
according to His glorious power,
for all patience and longsuffering with joy.
COLOSSIANS 1:10–11

*B*e careful which habits
you choose. They can either become
your power or your prison.

___

God is faithful, who will not allow you to be
tempted beyond what you are able,
but with the temptation will also make the way of escape,
that you may be able to bear it.
1 Corinthians 10:13

A life of godly obedience results in a life of inner tranquility.

—

If they obey and serve Him,
they shall spend their days in prosperity,
and their years in pleasure.
JOB 36:11

Be always alert.
Only the comfortable are
caught unawares.

Be sober, be vigilant;
because your adversary the devil walks
about like a roaring lion,
seeking whom he may devour.
1 PETER 5:8

*T*he secret of contentment
lies not in possessing many things
but in wanting few things.

———

Better is little with righteousness,
than vast revenues without justice.
PROVERBS 16:8

To live a great life,
serve a great God.

—

Call to Me, and I will answer you,
and show you great and might things,
which you do not know.
JEREMIAH 33:3

$\mathcal{T}$he secret to being a generous
Christian in public is being
a committed disciple in secret.

———

But you, when you pray, go into your room,
and when you have shut your door,
pray to your Father who is in the secret place;
and your Father who sees
in secret will reward you openly.
MATTHEW 6:6

*E*ven a turtle has to stick out
its neck if it wants to move ahead.
God will show you the general
direction you must travel,
but the specifics
of the journey are up to you.

I am the LORD your God,
who teaches you to profit,
who leads you by the way you should go.
ISAIAH 48:17

*R*esentment never did
anybody any good.
Find peace by
forgiving and forgetting.

Be angry, and do not sin:
do not let the sun go down on your wrath.
EPHESIANS 4:26

It takes courage to say "no"
to sinful suggestions.

———

Be of good courage,
and He shall strengthen your heart,
all you who hope in the LORD.
PSALM 31:24

*H*olding onto anger
is like holding
onto a snake—
slippery and dangerous.

———

Do not hasten in your spirit to be angry,
for anger rests in the bosom of fools.
ECCLESIASTES 7:9

A little extra effort now
results in tremendous payoffs
down the road.

There is gold and a multitude of rubies,
but the lips of knowledge are a precious jewel.
PROVERBS 20:15

$\mathcal{L}$earn to look at life
with a smile.
Find the joke and
pass it on to other folks.

He who loves purity of heart
and has grace on his lips,
the king will be his friend.
PROVERBS 22:11

God's tests are invariably true or false, not multiple choice.

The Jesus said to him,
"Away with you, Satan! For it is written,
You shall worship the Lord your God,
and Him only you shall serve."
MATTHEW 4:10

The road of sin and destruction
has many detours
but allows for few U-turns.

———

The Lord knows how to
deliver the godly out of temptations.
2 PETER 2:9

*N*o one will fault you for being too generous in life.

He who has a generous eye will be blessed,
for he gives of his bread to the poor.
PROVERBS 22:9

*N*ever build security on people
or things. Only the
all-powerful, ever-present God
can offer true security.

———

*I can do all things through Christ
who strengthens me.*
PHILIPPIANS 4:13

*P*eople with imagination and creativity are a rare commodity.

———

*Every good gift and
every perfect gift is from above,
and comes down
from the Father of lights.*
JAMES 1:17

*H*appiness fleets from
moment to moment,
but the joy that God gives
abides forever.

___

*Let those also who love
Your name be joyful in You.*
PSALM 5:11